Dedicated to the Chairman and Personification of Cool and Nice, Gabriel Lovas 😎

. . . and to all the cool and nice people around the world.

Spread kindness like butter...everywhere. 💕

Happiness is something when you give it away, you end up having more. 🎵

© MMXVII BCBN LTD/DELICIOUS LTD.

An imprint of Bonnier Publishing USA
251 Park Avenue South, New York, NY 10010
All rights reserved, including the right of reproduction in whole or in part in any form.
SIZZLE PRESS is a trademark of Bonnier Publishing USA, and associated
colophon is a trademark of Bonnier Publishing USA.

Designed by BCBN Design.
Curation and additional design by Chaos Fashion.
Cover image of Leo Lovingtons by the legendary Marc Newson.
Special design thanks to Lenny Kravitz and Kirsten Mattila at Kravitz Design,
Pat McGrath at Pat McGrath Labs, and BCBN design master Dan Sheffield.
Special thanks to Al MacCuish and the Sunshine Company.
All characters, text and content © BCBN LTD.

Printed and bound in China.
First Edition

2 4 6 8 10 9 7 5 3 1

Library of Congress Cataloging-in-Publication Data is available upon request.
ISBN 978-1-4998-0711-0
sizzlepressbooks.com
bonnierpublishingusa.com

BE COOL BE NICE

Be Cool Be Nice is not just a book . . . (as you can see from the cool and nice interactive cover with singing and rapping 3-D Cool Leo). 🐻
The *Be Cool Be Nice App* is free . . . 😎 because the best things in life are free and worth sharing like joy, laughter, pizza (oops . . . pizza is not free, but our BCBN app is).
The BCBN app can be used on most iPhone, iPad, or Android devices. It is easy to use and is unlike anything you have experienced before. Simply download from iTunes or Google Play (you will need an internet connection 📶 to do this) and scan the pages with the icon above.

The *Be Cool Be Nice App* will allow you to:
- View exclusive videos from some of the amazing designer contributors to these wonderful pages.
- Watch special messages ✉ from some of the coolest and nicest superstars. ✨
- Listen and watch the BCBN music video. 🎵
- Discover and complete interactive activities from the pages of the book. Take a selfie with the BCBN face filters of Cool Leo and Popsi Cool, and share with friends.
- Photograph your coolest and nicest friends using the selfie booth and nominate them for the BCBN award. 🏆
- Spread the BCBN message by sharing exclusive digital stickers and postcards on social media from the main app menu.

Have Fun!
#BeCoolBeNice

Unlock BCBN'S
Snapchat lens

This book is only for boys and girls, men and women, and the occasional dog, bear, cat, honeybee and popsicle (plus their friends, relatives and acquaintances where deemed absolutely necessary). It is strictly forbidden to anyone under the age of 1 or over the age of 165.

INTRO

If you are experiencing Chronic Bad Attitude Syndrome (BAS) from any friends and relations, please give them this book immediately with the appropriate pages highlighted for the avoidance of doubt and error and/or potential jail time post haste.

It is especially recommended for teens and young adults, old people, fat people, skinny people, and in-touch-with-their-inner-child people. It is absolutely not recommended for any people over 11 feet 7 inches tall or dinosaurs.

If you are experiencing drama in the workplace, please refer to page 38.

If you are being bullied at school or work, please see page 30.

If you have a serious selfie addiction, please see pages 28, 82 and 83.

If you are experiencing Chronic Bad Attitude Syndrome (CBAS) yourself, please refer to the User Guide on pages 10 and 11, and follow the instructions to the letter post haste.

USER GUIDE

FOR OPTIMUM RESULTS, READ
BE COOL BE NICE EVERY DAY
FOR AT LEAST TWO WEEKS,
THEN...

1. MEMORIZE one verse each day (21 days)

2. SHARE your favorite verses with family, friends and acquaintances old and new by spoken word (not only via text, email or social media)

3. PUT the words in the verses to practical use in your every day activities

4. SAY thank you every single time someone does something nice for you

5. WATCH how people around you respond to you more positively

6. LOOK at how many more doors of opportunity and possibility open to you

7. LISTEN more than you speak

8. LEARN how to be kinder everyday

9. FEEL how good you feel every day when you are more gracious and grateful

10. SEE how everything gets better and better even when things do not first appear so

11. PAY forward your blessings by being cool and nice to as many people as possible

12. ENJOY as your blessings multiply

* Remove the stickers from the front and back cover ...
then personalize your BCBN book using our super
cool and nice stickers. Share on social media. Have Fun!
#BeCoolBeNice

THIS BOOK BELONGS TO

· ·

BE COOL
BE NICE

NOT JUST ONCE
NOT JUST TWICE
WITH EVERYTHING
YOU DO OR SAY
KINDNESS TAKES
YOU ALL THE WAY

A GENTLE MANNER DOES NO HARM
A LITTLE GRACE, A LITTLE CHARM
GRATITUDE WINS YOU THE PRIZE
IT'S SIMPLE WHEN YOU REALIZE

Every little thing you do

ENDS UP COMING
BACK TO YOU
✈

#KarmaComin'AtYa

IT ALL BEGINS
WITH EASY RULES
TO GET YOU THROUGH
HERE ARE THE TOOLS!

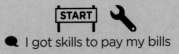

START

I got skills to pay my bills

COMPLICATED IT IS NOT
THE PERFECT WAY TO FEEL ON TOP

IS WHEN YOU RISE BE GLAD HOORAY!
SAY THANK YOU FOR ANOTHER DAY

THANK YOU FOR ANOTHER DAY

Rise and shine porcupine

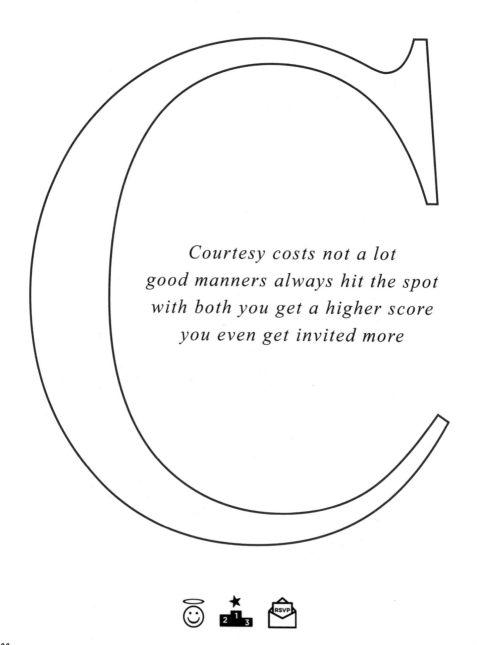

Courtesy costs not a lot
good manners always hit the spot
with both you get a higher score
you even get invited more

#checkitb4uwreckit

Think

BEFORE YOUR WORDS COME OUT

& *if you are*

IN ANY

DOUBT

THINK AGAIN

THEN HOLD THEM BACK IN CASE

they may TO

SEEM O ATTACK

When writing
I would recommend
to check it twice
before you send,
before the flames
you do ignite,
be sure the sentiment
is right ...

SELFIE IS
AS SELFIE DOES
A PICTURE
MAGNIFIES WHAT WAS
BEFORE YOU POST
HASTE NOT MY DEAR
LEST TROUBLE BUBBLES
DO APPEAR

Once you post snaps, can't ever go back

A BULLY
IS A COWARD TRUE
IGNORE WHAT
THEY MAY SAY OR DO
RISE ABOVE
THIS TOO SHALL PASS
THEN YOU'LL BE FIRST
AND THEY'LL BE LAST

Anyone seen Robin?!
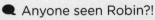

1 2 3 4 5 6

AS YOU WOULD
HAVE DONE TO YOU
UNTO OTHERS
SAME BE TRUE
JUST BEFORE
YOU CLOSE THE DEAL
ASK, HOW WOULD
THIS MAKE ME FEEL?

#Major!

PLEASE IS STILL THE MAGIC WORD
IT SELDOM FAILS WHEN IT IS HEARD
A WINNER NEVER NEEDS TO FLAUNT
ARROGANCE IS JUST A FRONT

WHEN SOMEONE TAKES
YOUR BLUES AWAY
SEND THEM A MESSAGE
TO CONVEY
HOW MUCH IT MEANT
THEN UNDENIED
YOUR BLESSINGS
THEY WILL MULTIPLY

#BounteousBlessings

WHEN DRAMA SAYS
COME OUT AND PLAY
TURN AND RUN
THE OTHER WAY
BEFORE YOU GET
INTO A FIGHT
TWO WRONGS
WILL NEVER MAKE
ONE RIGHT

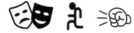

🗨 Kitty, you in danger girl
#MyTailDon'tStingThat'sJustBling

If feelings, skin or bone be torn
By something that is said or done
Sorry said, sincerely meant
Diminishes the incident

When sorry isn't quite enough
To pacify the waters rough
Forgiveness makes the troubles melt
A gift bestowed unto yourself

#WordDuJour
#Sorry

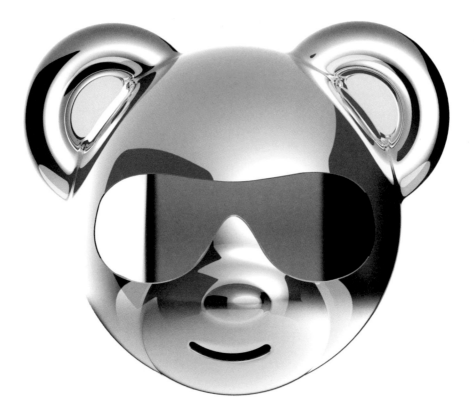

#ReflectionAffection

WITH WHOM YOU
CHOOSE TO STAY
AND LET NO ONE
LEAD YOU ASTRAY
A SMILING FACE
DO NOT CONFUSE
FOR ALWAYS GOOD
IN CASE YOU LOSE

#Don'tThrowShadeBoo

INSTEAD OF BEING
THE VOICE OF GLOOM
WHEREVER YOU GO
LIGHT UP THE ROOM
GRUMPY BOOTS
NO FRIENDS HE'S GOT
HAPPY FACE
SHE'S GOT A LOT

NOT

FOR OTHER ONES

TO BLAME

YOU HOLD THE KEY

TO WIN THE GAME

IN SEARCH OF

MIRACLES TO VIEW

THE MAGIC

IS INSIDE OF YOU

47

If something is meant to be yours
It will be with you in due course
More sure a bet than instant fame
Keep your word, honor your name

If they ain't fun... run hon!

GO WHERE
YOU ARE CELEBRATED
NOT WHERE
YOU ARE TOLERATED
BELIEVE A PERSON
WHEN THEY SHOW YOU
WHO THEY ARE
THE FIRST TIME
WON'T YOU?

THESE GOLDEN RULES
FOR LIFE AND MORE
WHEN FOLLOWED
THERE WOULD BE NO WAR
OR OTHER GRISLY
TALES TO TELL
THE SUREST WAY
TO JOY AND HEALTH...

#LetLoveRule

BE STEADY
UPRIGHT
DIGNIFIED

THOUGHTFULNESS
PERSONIFIED

YOU WANT YOUR RICHES
MAGNIFIED?

#Thoughtful

#NuffSaid

YOUR WORK
HERE IS NOT
DONE SUN
SHINE 😎

NOW COMES

THE FUN... ➡️

QUIZ

CIRCLE THE LETTER FOR EACH VERSE OF THE BOOK THAT IS MOST CORRECT FOR YOU. DO YOU FOLLOW LEO, FRU AND POPSI COOL'S ADVICE IN EACH VERSE?

BE COOL BE NICE
NOT JUST ONCE NOT JUST TWICE
WITH EVERYTHING YOU DO OR SAY
KINDNESS TAKES YOU ALL THE WAY

A   B   C   D   E

A GENTLE MANNER DOES NO HARM
A LITTLE GRACE A LITTLE CHARM
GRATITUDE WINS YOU THE PRIZE
IT'S SIMPLE WHEN YOU REALIZE

A   B   C   D   E

THAT EVERY LITTLE THING YOU DO
ENDS UP COMING BACK TO YOU
IT ALL BEGINS WITH EASY RULES
TO GET YOU THROUGH HERE ARE THE TOOLS

A   B   C   D   E

COMPLICATED IT IS NOT
THE PERFECT WAY TO FEEL ON TOP
IS WHEN YOU RISE BE GLAD HOORAY!
SAY THANK YOU FOR ANOTHER DAY

A   B   C   D   E

COURTESY COSTS NOT A LOT
GOOD MANNERS ALWAYS HIT THE SPOT
WITH BOTH YOU GET A HIGHER SCORE
YOU EVEN GET INVITED MORE

A   B   C   D   E

THINK BEFORE YOUR WORDS COME OUT
AND IF YOU ARE IN ANY DOUBT
THINK AGAIN THEN HOLD THEM BACK
IN CASE THEY MAY SEEM TO ATTACK

A   B   C   D   E

WHEN WRITING I WOULD RECOMMEND
TO CHECK IT TWICE BEFORE YOU SEND
BEFORE THE FLAMES YOU DO IGNITE
BE SURE THE SENTIMENT IS RIGHT

A   B   C   D   E

SELFIE IS AS SELFIE DOES
A PICTURE MAGNIFIES WHAT WAS
BEFORE YOU POST HASTE NOT MY DEAR
LEST TROUBLE BUBBLES DO APPEAR

A   B   C   D   E

A BULLY IS A COWARD TRUE
IGNORE WHAT THEY MAY SAY OR DO
RISE ABOVE, THIS TOO SHALL PASS
THEN YOU'LL BE FIRST AND THEY'LL BE LAST

A   B   C   D   E

AS YOU WOULD HAVE DONE TO YOU
UNTO OTHERS SAME BE TRUE
JUST BEFORE YOU CLOSE THE DEAL
ASK, HOW WOULD THIS MAKE ME FEEL?

A   B   C   D   E

PLEASE IS STILL THE MAGIC WORD
IT SELDOM FAILS WHEN IT IS HEARD
A WINNER NEVER NEEDS TO FLAUNT
ARROGANCE IS JUST A FRONT

A   B   C   D   E

WHEN SOMEONE TAKES YOUR BLUES AWAY
SEND THEM A MESSAGE TO CONVEY
HOW MUCH IT MEANT THEN UNDENIED
YOUR BLESSINGS THEY WILL MULTIPLY

A   B   C   D   E

A. EVERY TIME

B. OFTEN

C. SOMETIMES

D. ONLY WHEN I WANT SOMETHING

E. NEVER

SOME ARE WITH YOU FOR A SEASON
YOU SHOULD BE THERE FOR A REASON
MAKE THE MOST OF WHAT YOU'VE GOT
FROM YOUR NEIGHBOR COVET NOT

A **B** C D E

WHEN DRAMA SAYS COME OUT AND PLAY
TURN AND RUN THE OTHER WAY
BEFORE YOU GET INTO A FIGHT
TWO WRONGS WILL NEVER MAKE ONE RIGHT

A **B** C D E

BEWARE WITH WHOM YOU CHOOSE TO STAY
AND LET NO ONE LEAD YOU ASTRAY
A SMILING FACE DO NOT CONFUSE
FOR ALWAYS GOOD, IN CASE YOU LOSE

A **B** C D E

INSTEAD OF BEING THE VOICE OF GLOOM
WHEREVER YOU GO LIGHT UP THE ROOM
GRUMPY BOOTS NO FRIENDS HE'S GOT
HAPPY FACE SHE'S GOT A LOT

A **B** C D E

LOOK NOT FOR OTHER ONES TO BLAME
YOU HOLD THE KEY TO WIN THE GAME
IN SEARCH OF MIRACLES TO VIEW?
THE MAGIC IS INSIDE OF YOU

A **B** C D E

IF SOMETHING IS MEANT TO BE YOURS
IT WILL BE WITH YOU IN DUE COURSE
MORE SURE A BET THAN INSTANT FAME
KEEP YOUR WORD, HONOR YOUR NAME

A **B** C D E

GO WHERE YOU ARE CELEBRATED
NOT WHERE YOU ARE TOLERATED
BELIEVE A PERSON WHEN THEY SHOW YOU
WHO THEY ARE THE FIRST TIME, WON'T YOU?

A **B** C D E

THESE GOLDEN RULES FOR LIFE AND MORE
WHEN FOLLOWED THERE WOULD BE NO WAR
OR OTHER GRISLY TALES TO TELL
THE QUICKEST WAY TO JOY AND HEALTH . . .

A **B** C D E

BE STEADY, UPRIGHT, DIGNIFIED
THOUGHTFULNESS PERSONIFIED
YOU WANT YOUR RICHES MAGNIFIED?
BE YOU, BE COOL, BE NICE

A **B** C D E

RESULTS

A If you answered mostly A
you are the coolest and nicest

B If you answered mostly B
you are cool and nice

C If you answered mostly C
you need to read this book
every day for 2 months

D If you answered mostly D
you need to read this book
every day for 6 months

E If you answered mostly E
you need to turn yourself in...Quick!

WHAT DOES COOL MEAN TO YOU?

Use images, phrases and words to express what 'cool' means to you, but please remember Boo–being cool is how you are, not what you wear. #nice-is-cool

WORDS

PHRASES

IMAGES

Share on social #BeCoolBeNice

No
ARTIFICIAL FLAVOR

100%
REALNESS

59

From Manner to Manor!

GOOD MANNERS ARE LIKE
A VIP ALL-ACCESS PASS
AND A FREE UPGRADE
TO FIRST CLASS...

KINDNESS OPENS THE DOORS
TO ENDLESS POSSIBILITIES.
YOU CAN CHANGE SOMEONE'S MOOD, DAY, LIFE
(AND YOURS TOO)
WHEN YOU MAKE THEM FEEL
RESPECTED AND APPRECIATED
*USING ONE OF THE BCBN POSTCARDS INCLUDED
IN THIS BOOK, WRITE YOUR OWN TOP 10
MANNERS TIPS AND SHARE WITH YOUR
BESTIE AND ON SOCIAL MEDIA #BECOOLBENICE
#MANNER-IT-UP-BOO

63

GRATITUDE ATTITUDE 😊

Make a list of the things you are most grateful for each day, like the sunshine, your home, your health, your soon to be abundant wealth (after reading and sharing this book) 😊 #GratitudeAttitude

1. _____

2. _____

3. _____

4. _____

5. _____

6. _____

7. _____

8. _____

9. _____

10. _____

Now take your Gratitude Attitude list further, by using inspiration from the subjects on the next two pages

• Share on social media something you are grateful for every day . . . for a whole month!

• For example, on the first day of the month, share a snap of a friend you are grateful for and explain why.

• On the second day, share an image of a family member you are grateful for, and explain why. Sharing is caring.

Focus on the things you do have instead of the things you don't.

#GratitudeAttitude

Gratitude Sharing

1 Friend

2 Family

3 When You Wake Up

4 Sound

5 Taste

6 Smell

7 Song

8 Small Thing

9 Big Thing

10 Memory

11 Place

12 Holiday

13 Mentor

14 Talents

15 Opportunity

Share each day, on social media, something or someone you are grateful for, using the subjects above for inspiration.
Go to page 138 for examples. #BeCoolBeNice

Monthly Challenge

16 Tradition

17 Health

18 Act Of Kindness From A Stranger

19 Home

20 Challenge

21 Possession

22 Your Magic

23 Loyal Person

24 Kind Person

25 Job/School

26 Time

27 Gift From The Universe

28 Lesson You Are Grateful For

29 Words Of Wisdom

30 #BCBN

#SharingIsCaring

Every Little Thing You Do...

NICE THINGS YOU CAN DO

List the cool and nice things you can do. Brighten someone's day with a nice gesture or a compliment. Then write the nice things that have also been done for you and watch the blessings multiply.

NICE THINGS DONE FOR YOU

Remember, every little thing you do ends up coming back to you! #KarmaComin'AtYa

KARMA COMIN' AT YA

Karma 'Ka:me'
*noun - the sum of a person's actions, viewed as deciding
their fate in the future*

Make a note of the things you did or said that
you feel sorry for, like when you lost your cool with
someone, when you drop-kicked your neighbor's cat,
when you maybe threw a little bit too much shade.

#Don'tThrowShadeBoo #KarmaComin'AtYa

Throwing shade: When throwing shade, it is almost
always obvious to others that the thrower, not the
throwee is the unkind one (unless you are dealing
with an expert shade thrower) . . . #SideEye
Passive Aggressive = the weakest form of shade
#Checkitb4Uwreckit

KARMA BOOMERANG

Color in your BCBN
Karma Boomerang.
Throw that kindness
and positivity around
everywhere.

Once completed, share
your Karma Boomerang
on social using the
hashtag #BeCoolBeNice

BCBN · BCBN · BCBN · BCBN

Thank You For Another Day

Thank you is a magic phrase in any language. There are many different ways to show you are thankful . . . use them freely and often.

Спасибо
Spasibo
(spuh-SEE-buh)
RUSSIAN

благодаря
Blagodarya
(blagodaria)
BULGARIAN

Dhanyavād
(thun-yuh-vod)
HINDI

Mahalo
(ma-HA-lo)
HAWAIIAN

Ngiyabonga
ZULU

Tack
SWEDISH

고맙습니다
(Gamsahamnida)
KOREAN

Terima Kasih
(tuh-REE-mah KAH-see)
INDONESIAN

obrigado [m] / obrigada [f]
(oh-bree-GAH-doo /
oh-bree-GAH-dah)
PORTUGUESE

Баярлалаа
(bayarlalaa)
MONGOLIAN

Big Ups

Diolch
(Dee-all'CH)
WELSH

Dank je
(DAHNK yuh)
DUTCH

Gracias
(GRAH-syahs)
SPANISH

I WOULD LIKE TO 🎭
THANK THE ACADEMY

Now it is your turn to thank anyone and everyone who has lifted you up. List the people below that you would like to thank and why. Make your thank you speech fab!

_____

_____

_____

_____

_____

_____

Now you have your fab list, nominate at least three of these people who are the epitome of all things cool and nice for the BCBN award! 🏆

Use the BCBN app to take a photo 📷 of your nominee holding the BCBN award and share using the hashtag #BeCoolBeNiceNominee.

Encourage them to nominate people of their own and watch the cool and nice appreciation celebration grow! ✉

#SharingIsCaring

BCBN AWARD

BE COOL BE NICE™

75

COMPLIMENT SUPPLEMENT

Be complimentary! Pay someone a compliment, whether friend, family or stranger . . . it may be just the thing that brightens up their day.

Make a compliment list for your friends and family and watch as the smiles multiply (yours and theirs).

#COMPLIMENTS OF THE HOUSE

Share the love on social media #BeCoolBeNice

BE COURTEOUS

Take the blue courtesy bus to happy 🙂 trails...

List at least 10 ways you can be courteous, e.g. opening the door for someone, letting someone overtake in traffic, not telling someone they look fat in that hat...

1. _____

2. _____

3. _____

4. _____

5. _____

6. _____

7. _____

8. _____

9. _____

10. _____

#Kindness-is-free

#ReminderToBeKinder

SAY **No** TO NINCOMPOOPERY

nincompoop |'ninkem, poop'|
noun — a foolish person

TACT FACT

tact |'takt'|
noun — sensitivity in dealing with others*

A keen sense of what to say or do to avoid giving offense; skill in dealing with difficult or delicate situations.

STICKS AND STONES

'Sticks and stones may hurt my bones but words will never harm me' is a big fat fib (probably one of the biggest fibs ever told).

We all know that words can sting more than pepper in the eye and the wounds can last an eternity.

Watch your mouth or wash your mouth . . . before you have to take it back, have some tact.

FIX IT UP

Write down in one side of the heart when you may have said or done something untactful. Then in the other side, write what you can say or do to make that person feel better and the heart whole.

TACTFUL

UNTACTFUL

SAFE SELFIE CHECKLIST

A PICTURE MAGNIFIES WHAT WAS... CHECK IT BEFORE YOU WRECK IT!

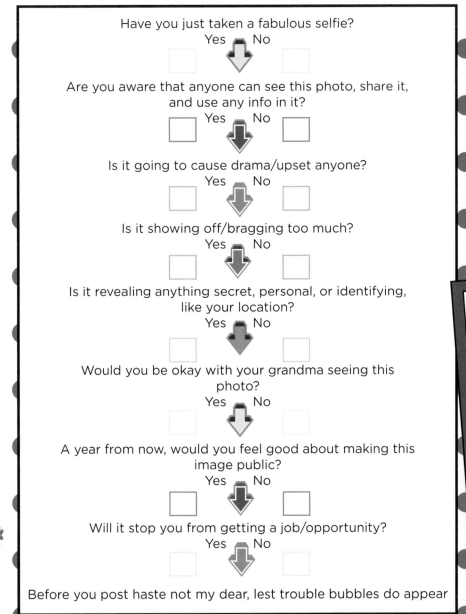

Have you just taken a fabulous selfie?

Yes ⬇ No

Are you aware that anyone can see this photo, share it, and use any info in it?

Yes ⬇ No

Is it going to cause drama/upset anyone?

Yes ⬇ No

Is it showing off/bragging too much?

Yes ⬇ No

Is it revealing anything secret, personal, or identifying, like your location?

Yes ⬇ No

Would you be okay with your grandma seeing this photo?

Yes ⬇ No

A year from now, would you feel good about making this image public?

Yes ⬇ No

Will it stop you from getting a job/opportunity?

Yes ⬇ No

Before you post haste not my dear, lest trouble bubbles do appear

SELFIE 📷

SCRAPBOOK

Now you have seen the Safe Selfie Checklist, use this page to make a Selfie Scrapbook. First scan the page with the BCBN app and take a selfie using the Cool Leo🐻 and Popsi Cool filters. Use only 'cool' and 'nice' photos!

Add your photo within the lines

Add your photo within the lines

Add your photo within the lines

Add your photo within the lines

Add your photo within the lines

Add your photo within the lines

Add your photo within the lines

Add your photo within the lines

Turn The Frown
əpᴉsdՈ Down

Put a positive spin on it! Sometimes it is easier to focus on the bad and then we miss out on the good. Match the negative to the positive words below.

glass half-empty

coward

polite

thoughtless

boring

relaxed

thoughtful

sweet

anxious

gratitude

kind

happy

tact

dull

stressed

ungrateful

selfish

ignorance

rude

rough

generous

unkind

glass half-full

tactless

brave

calm

bitter   intelligence

ungracious

exciting

gracious   smooth

sad   brilliant

Spot The Positives

Find the cool and nice words in the BCBN word search, and remember that positivity can be found in any situation. #SilverLining #ThisTooShallPass

becoolbenice
happy ☺
calm
conscientious
karma
light 💡

manners
gentle
grace
charm
gratitude
thanks ✋

courtesy
think 💭
please
tact
believe
coolleo 🐻

l	o	r	t	a	c	t	l	n	m	z	e	p	c	e
z	b	o	b	i	k	t	j	a	g	c	g	i	o	f
c	o	n	s	c	i	e	n	t	i	o	u	s	u	a
k	g	f	k	g	e	n	a	n	v	v	l	m	r	z
a	a	r	c	n	e	l	e	g	s	z	f	l	t	g
r	y	l	a	r	i	b	n	k	v	c	o	n	e	d
m	l	a	s	t	l	h	n	a	p	l	e	a	s	e
a	h	i	o	o	i	a	t	g	b	t	i	g	y	a
y	w	a	o	e	h	t	r	m	e	h	s	e	o	l
g	l	c	p	t	l	a	u	e	v	e	i	l	e	b
m	e	i	v	p	c	l	h	d	p	t	m	t	i	h
b	l	s	p	e	y	z	o	m	e	h	f	n	i	h
y	a	m	r	a	h	c	l	o	u	g	m	e	t	q
s	n	n	d	j	r	a	d	e	c	i	x	g	k	e
o	e	h	q	a	c	m	m	w	a	l	t	h	x	y

COMMON SENSE IS NOT AS COMMON AS IT SHOULD BE

It should be common sense that it's cool to be nice and to treat everyone as well as we wish to be treated. If only it were that simple.

DO YOU HAVE COMMON SENSE?

Complete the quiz, and find out! 🐝

Treat people the same way you would like to be treated
A. Always   B. Sometimes   C. Never

Check it twice before you send a text or email
A. Always   B. Sometimes   C. Never

Think before your words come out
A. Always   B. Sometimes   C. Never

You can win friends and influence people by being cool and nice
A. Always   B. Sometimes   C. Never

Having a gratitude attitude makes you happier
A. Always   B. Sometimes   C. Never

Causing drama brings you more drama and trouble bubbles
A. Always   B. Sometimes   C. Never

Believe a person when they show you who they are the first time won't you?
A. Always   B. Sometimes   C. Never

Go where you are celebrated, not where you are tolerated
A. Always   B. Sometimes   C. Never

If you answered mostly A you are wonderfully sensible
If you answered mostly B you are sometimes sensible but could use a bit extra
If you answered mostly C you need to check yourself before you wreck yourself...fast!

DUDE, DON'T BE RUDE

DON'T BE MEAN, DON'T BE RUDE
DO NOT HAVE AN ATTITUDE
KEEP YOUR ANGER TO YOURSELF
BLAME IT NOT ON SOMEONE ELSE

TURN THE FURY THAT YOU'RE FEELING
INTO SOMETHING MORE APPEALING

THE RAGE YOU STAGE SHOWS WHO YOU ARE
FROM YOUR DISPLAY
THEY WILL STAY FAR

NO ONE WANTS A GRUMPY GROUCH
WITH TEMPER TANTRUMS ON THEIR COUCH

HIDE THE MOANER, ZIP HIS MOUTH
THEN WHEN HE'S HAPPY ☺, LET HIM OUT

HAVE A PRIVATE INNER CHAT
BE COOL AND NICE
THAT'S WHERE IT'S AT 😎

*HASHTAG THAT!

Simmer Down Boo!

With every new advance in technology comes ever more efficient ways to be as mean as a big bag of ugly to each other. Just because you woke up on the wrong side of the air mattress, stepped in cat's pee and are having the baddest of bad hair days does not give you license to act the fool with folks.

SIMMER DOWN BOO! . . . and repress your inner No No Gang. Keep your bad side in check with these easy tools:

Cage the Rage by...
Breathing deeply
Counting to ten
Meditating

Avoid A Temper Tantrum at all costs!
Rise above, this too shall pass.
Avoid those situations which may push your anger buttons

Let it All Out . . . the RIGHT way!
Exercise! Let out your rage in a proactive and healthy way: in competitive sports, or by hitting a punching bag. Don't bottle up the rage, run a few laps and sweat it out and if all else fails, let loose into a pillow, not a person (or a cat)!

BE CIVIL

civilization = civilized = civility

ci·vil·i·ty |'se'vɪleti'|
noun — formal politeness and courtesy in behavior or speech.

Forget the uncivil behavior we see on reality TV and in the news, that is definitely not the way to be.

Even the ancient caveman eventually figured out that he would not get into the club by clubbing everyone over the head. He needed to learn civility.

There is an old saying: you can catch more bees with honey than with vinegar.

We may not want to catch bees, but we do want a sweet and happy life.

Everyone has feelings, so treat others as you would like to be treated . . .

"I hope we can treat each other with civility and respect"

synonyms: courtesy, courteousness, politeness, good manners, graciousness, consideration, respect,
"he treated me with civility"

Honey Bee Cool

The waiter, the skater, the doctor, the baker, the beggar, the butler, the candlestick maker. Everyone of every shape, color, origin, religion or non-religion; they all have the same need to be treated with civility . . . just like you.

Just because there may be a 'machine' between us and the other person—whether it's a car, a phone, social status, or the internet—it should not take away the humanity of the other person. If we are in traffic, it's not another car we are screaming at, it's another person. If we are on social media, it's not a machine we are trolling, it's another person; like someone's sister, brother, mother or significant other . . . so best that we resist the urge to do or say something mean as the next time, that person could be . . . you

#KarmaComin'AtYa

Civil List

List the ways that you can be more civil in your day-to-day life.

Make a mental note of when you have been uncivil and list the different ways this can be improved.

Were you dismissive to a waiter?

Did you disregard someone because you felt they were not sufficiently 'important?'

Did you honk your horn at someone in traffic?

List it, then fix it!

#NoRoadRage

_____

_____

_____

_____

_____

_____

_____

There
is no
civilization
without
civility

BE COOL BE NICE

Neville Jacobs Interview

Q. Social media has made it incredibly easy to bully people. What would your message be to all the trolls/cyber bullies?
A. Spend less time online and more time connecting with dogs (or people).

Q. What is a kindness/good manners tool that you learned that would also be valuable for others?
A. Give more hugs, receive more hugs. I get a lot of affection at home and in the office, so I try to give back as much as I get.

Q. How do you think we can all improve being cool and nice in our daily lives?
A. Say please and thank you and hold open doors for others.

Q. Have you or someone you know ever been bullied? How did this make them/you feel?
A. When I was a puppy, older dogs tried to bully me in the park. It's ironic given that I'm a Bull Terrier (don't prejudge because of a name or breed). It didn't bother me too much then and it doesn't bother me now because I'm proud of who I am and you should be proud of who you are too.

Q. What advice would you give them/yourself now?
A. Life is a journey with ebbs and flows. Good dogs (and people) come and good people go. Be kind to yourself and be kind to others. This is your life to live, so don't live it for others.

Q. What made you want to support Be Cool Be Nice?
A. Be Cool Be Nice is a reminder to consider others and to pause and think before you criticize, judge or speak ill of anyone.

Q. Who are the coolest and nicest people you know (historical or otherwise)?
A. My dad, Marc Jacobs.

Q. What positive words would you use to describe yourself?
A. Kind. Patient. Goofy.

nevillejacobs

35w

♥ 6,691 likes
nevillejacobs BE COOL BE NICE 💙

@nevillejacobs

#WeLoveNeville

BCBN QUOTES:

It's cool to be cool and it's nice to be nice. So, be cool be nice! I've been fortunate enough to meet some of the most amazing and talented people all over the world and the one thing they all have in common are these two qualities. Kindness never goes out of style and the beautiful *Be Cool Be Nice* book is a wonderful reminder of this.

Kylie Minogue - Performer/Icon

I think Be Cool Be Nice is one of the most important things, especially right now. To be kind to each other is truly infectious. In this time of fear and disconnect and internet, we need to remind each other that kindness is the only way.

Zoe Kravitz - Actress/Performer

Be Cool Be Nice because we have to let love rule.

Lenny Kravitz - Rock Star

People only bully because they themselves are in pain, therefore I ask all bullies to consider the fact that they are inflicting the same pain they are experiencing on someone else and they are continuing the cycle. Instead, seek help and talk to someone you feel safe with about what you're going through.

June Sarpong - Broadcaster/Philanthropist/Author of *Diversify*

I have always believed that you get back from the world what you put into it. If you spend all day making others feel miserable online or via social media, then chances are you are not experiencing life to the full. With that in mind, I invite anyone who has ever left a disparaging or bullying comment in cyberspace to challenge themselves to go one week without doing or saying anything negative online - and then step back and watch how much better their own lives become because they are no longer spreading toxicity. That one week can then turn into a lifetime of positivity.

Pat McGrath - The Number 1 Makeup Artist In The World

Treat others in the way that you would like to be treated. Respond to unkindness with kindness. You can do no wrong by showing people love.

Aida Cable - The Royal Foundation of the Duke and Duchess of Cambridge and Prince Harry

The coolest way to be is nice. Be Cool Be Nice is a fun and important motto, especially for young people. When you can reach out and be kind to another person that is what life is all about.

HRH Princess Beatrice

I would tell the 9-year-old Alex, who felt pretty powerless and voiceless, that one day that thing that made you different will be celebrated, it will be cool and one day you will go on to meet the Queen.

Alex Holmes - Head of the Diana Award Anti-Bullying Campaign

Do at least one cool and nice thing every day for someone else - a random act of kindness. Imagine if everyone did?! 7 billion positive interactions each day . . . now that's a cool and nice world.

David Ohana - UNICEF

At a time when, across the world, we are seeing the impact of a loss of tolerance, we all need to stand up and raise our voices against bullying and unkind behavior. That is the key message of this book. The importance of civility and respect. We all have a right to be treated with dignity. It is a message that not only children but adults need to hear and act on. This book reminds us all that each and every one of us must play our part to create a more just society. The message is simple, the impact profound.

The Rt Hon The Baroness Amos - Director of SOAS, University of London, Former United Nations Undersecretary General for Humanitarian Affairs and Leader of the House of Lords

Do a good or kind deed and it boomerangs back to you. Speed cameras watch our every move in a car, so just pretend you're being watched by deed camera, clocking your every kindness.

Be Cool Be Nice is a calm balm for the soul.

Kathy Lette - Bestselling Author

People say sticks and stones may break your bones but words will never hurt you . . . words do hurt. They can leave scars in many different shapes or forms. Be you, be cool, be nice.

Lucca - Student

We are all wonderfully different. Embrace who you are. Nobody deserves to be mistreated for being different, whatever those differences are. If bullied, we can choose to feel small, or we can rise above as the *Be Cool Be Nice* book says. Love every bit of you and to others Be Cool and Be Nice.

Imogen - Student

There will always be critical people in the world, but you don't have to be the type of person who is affected by harsh critics. Being aware that it is the bullies who feel bad about themselves can be empowering. The affirmation "I AM ENOUGH" is very useful.

Marisa Peer - Therapist and Author

Basic respect is so lacking these days, hence the increased incidence of bullying. We need to consider others' emotions and to think about how we would feel if someone did the same to us. Be Cool Be Nice applies to all ages and without prejudice cleverly manages to infuse messages which shape many of our basic values of respect for each other, irrespective of our differences.

Dr. Evadney Keith - General Medical Practitioner

YOUR GOOD AND BAD SIDE

We all have a good and bad side. 🎭

I have two naughty secret twins living in my head that I try to never let out, not even on special occasions. One is called Harold and one is called Bertha...you don't want to meet Harold or Bertha, especially not when they are hungry and trying to get to the buffet. 🍔

It is important for us all to keep our inner Harolds and Berthas locked 🔒 away from the community at large and to try to only let our inner sparkly light 💡 shine at all times. You never know what kind of rough day, week, month or life someone else is having, so best we not take our bad hair day out on them.

Not one of us is getting out of here alive (that in itself really makes us all equal)...so let's try to make the journey to the finish line as fun, free and fab as possible.

They won't say at your funeral, ☠ he had great shoes and a really cool car (at least let's hope not). People will remember you for how you made them feel, good or bad.

It's as simple as that. Be Cool Be Nice.

THE INFAMOUS
NoNo GANG

THIS CREW IS A BAD MUTHA...SHUT YOUR MOUTH

Name and design your own member of the NoNo Gang... and remember to keep them in check! Share your personal NoNo Gang member on social media using the hashtag #BeCoolBeNice

WANTED

BCBN·BCBN·BCBN·BCBN·BCBN

#Don'tThrowShadeBoo

JUDGE MENTAL 😝

Do not judge their clothes, their hair, their car, their chair . . . do not be judgmental.

Every time you want to say something judgmental, think again, then shut your boombox until you can think and say something happy. Don't be a smug bug and bring a dark cloud 💭 on someone's day. Put a smiley 😊 face on it.

Did you judge their height, their shoes, their weight, their news? Whichever and whoever you judged . . . write it down, then fix it up! (Make a list of who you judged and how you can make it better)

NO TROLL ZONE!

#NoTrollZone

It Is Not Coincidental

That the one who's most judgmental
tends to end up quite alone
(as) no one wants to hear them moan.

When we prejudge someone based on what they are
(gender, color, orientation, size, etc.)
rather than commend them for who they are
(kind, hilarious, talented, wise, etc.)... HA HA!
that is the lowest form of foolishness and ignorance...
that is the kind of ignorance that leads to
trouble and strife and stuff not nice,
for people and other living things.

To prejudge someone is to be prejudiced
To judge someone is to be judgmental.
Judge not your neighbor, friend or foe
Be Cool Be Nice ... is the way to go.

What do you love?

In order to not be led astray - know who you are.
Fill out the following questionnaire and learn a little bit
more about yourself - be honest, be brave!

Use four words to describe yourself.

....

What did you want to be when you were younger?

....

What do you want to be now?

....

What are you most proud of?

....

What is your biggest fear?

....

What in your life means the most?

....

What do you wish you did more of?

....

What piece of advice would you give yourself?

....

Do you have any regrets? If so, what and why?

....

If you could make someone's dreams come true – who
would they be and why?

....

What area of your life right now makes you the happiest?

....

No one can be you better than you.
Be You, Be Cool, Be Nice

Trouble Bubbles

FILL IN THE BUBBLES WITH
YOUR TROUBLES AND USE THE
BCBN APP TO MAKE THEM
POP AND DISAPPEAR!

RISE ABOVE

BE COOL BE NICE . . . IT WILL MAKE THE MEMORIES SWEETER AND THE RIDE SMOOTHER. HAPPY CRUISING!

MOVE ON

PROCESS AND EVALUATE

PROBLEM

GET COOL LEO OUT OF THE MAZE OF NEGATIVITY AND THROUGH TO THE OTHER SIDE, WHERE THE GRASS IS GREENER AND LIFE IS FUNNIER.

SHARE YOUR COMPLETED MAZE ON SOCIAL MEDIA WITH THE HASHTAG #BECOOLBENICE

APOLOGY CHRONOLOGY

What comes first, the chicken or the egg?
Who says sorry first?
He who dealt the first blow should cough up the apology with the quickness.

Say sorry . . . that one word can get you out of a lot of scrapes . . . use it freely (and quickly) when needed.

Write an 'I'm sorry' note to anyone you may have accidentally or purposely thrown under the bus.

ALL TIME APOLOGIES

For inspiration, check out the following with a little bit of popcorn and a lot of attention.

Elton John – 'Sorry Seems to Be the Hardest Word'
Justin Bieber – 'Sorry'
Frodo to Sam – The Lord Of The Rings
Elsa to Anna – Frozen
Chandler in the box to Joey – Friends
Simba to Mufasa – The Lion King
Ron to Harry and Hermione – Harry Potter
Darcy to Elizabeth – Pride and Prejudice
Kanye West to Taylor Swift
Kevin McCallister – Home Alone
Shrek to Donkey – Shrek
Aladdin to Abu – Aladdin
Adele – 'Hello'

I'M SORRY...

Make a creative list of the ways you can say sorry.
For example:
I must have really lost my marbles, I'm sorry.
(with bag or box of marbles) ●●●
I made a big mistake...I wish I could erase it. I'm sorry.
(with eraser) ◢
I was such a nut, I'm sorry.
(bag of nuts)
Please bear with me, I am sorry I was so stressed
with you.
(send them a pic of Cool Leo)
I really need to cool down, I am sorry I lost my temper.
(send them a pic of Popsi Cool)

WHEN WRITING I WOULD RECOMMEND
TO CHECK IT TWICE BEFORE YOU SEND
BEFORE THE FLAMES YOU DO IGNITE
BE SURE THE SENTIMENT IS RIGHT

Little Word/Big Meaning

FILL IN THE BLANKS . . .

LOVE ALL, TRUST A FEW, DO WRONG TO _____.
William Shakespeare

LOVE IS COMPOSED OF A SINGLE _____ INHABITING
TWO _____.
Aristotle

BEAUTY IS WHEN YOU CAN APPRECIATE _____. WHEN YOU
LOVE _____, THAT'S WHEN YOU'RE MOST BEAUTIFUL.
Zoe Kravitz

LOVE AND COMPASSION ARE _____, NOT LUXURIES.
WITHOUT THEM, HUMANITY CANNOT _____.
The Dalai Lama

KEEP AWAY FROM THOSE WHO TRY TO BELITTLE YOUR
_____. SMALL PEOPLE ALWAYS DO THAT, BUT THE REALLY
GREAT MAKE YOU BELIEVE THAT YOU TOO CAN BE _____.
Mark Twain

WHERE THERE IS LOVE, THERE IS _____.
Mahatma Gandhi

Empathy Symphony

Write a lyric on sharing someone's joy or pain.
Whether friend or stranger, we all hurt and heart
the same. #empathy

Video yourself performing your empathy symphony
and upload on social media using the hashtag
#BeCoolBeNice

Forgiveness Checklist

FORGIVENESS MAKES THE TROUBLES MELT, A GIFT BESTOWED UNTO YOURSELF...
LOOK AT THE FORGIVENESS CHECKLIST BELOW, AND TICK THEM OFF
AS YOU GO ALONG.

Have you said sorry with feeling and sincerity?

Yes   No

Have you put yourself in their shoes and questioned how your actions would make you feel?

Yes   No

Do you feel empathy?

Yes   No

Have you tried to make amends?

Yes   No

Have you learned from the mistake?

Yes   No

Have you applied what you have learned to another experience or situation?

Yes   No

#FORGIVE

Happiness Checklist

Happiness is a state of mind. To help you find your happy 😎 place, take some time to work through the happiness checklist.

You Time — whether that's relaxing in a bubble bath, going for a run or eating some ice cream 🍦 and watching a movie, take some time for yourself to just chill. 🍦

Pause — stop and reflect. Things can sometimes seem to be moving a hundred miles a minute, put your foot on the break and pause. #ThisTooShallPass 👍

Relax — treat yourself, meditate, take a walk in the park, play a fun game with your bestie❤, whatever makes you feel less stress.

Ditch the digital — and go old school, read a book 📖 or magazine and lose yourself in the stories. Color in a page in your *Be Cool Be Nice* journal and have a party being arty. ✏

Socialize — you time is great, but so is socializing. Meet up with friends, visit family and let the laughter flow. HA HA!

Sleep zzzzZ — you need your beauty sleep. A good night's rest does wonders for the mood and keeps the 'tude at bay.

FACE☺ VALUE

Don't take everything at face value. Turn this page upside down to see the hidden message and remember things are not always as they seem.

Sharing is Caring

Use your BCBN Photobooth and take a picture with your chosen cool and nice friend and share. Then stick the photo here and write all the reasons why you chose that person. Show them and make their day!

JOKES & STORIES

Write down fun and funny stories, and new jokes **HA HA!** so that when you step into the room, the smiles 😊 and laughter beam in with you. #LaughOutLoud

Share your BCBN jokes & stories on social!
#BeCoolBeNice

POPSI COOL'S HAPPY PLAYLIST

Chaka Khan – 'Ain't Nobody'

Aretha Franklin – 'I Say a Little Prayer'

Vanessa Paradis – 'Be My Baby'

Angie Stone – 'Life Story'

Ultra Nate – 'Free'

Stonebridge – 'Put 'Em High'

Stargate – 'Be Cool Be Nice (Remix)'

Miriam Makeba – 'Pata Pata'

Sérgio Mendes – 'Mas Que Nada'

Mocedades – 'Eres Tu'

Abba – 'Dancing Queen'

Beyoncé – 'Love on Top'

Lenny Kravitz – 'Fly Away'

Kylie Minogue – 'Love at First Sight'

Rita Ora – 'Grateful'

Katy Perry – 'Roar'

Wham! – 'Wake Me Up Before You Go-Go'

Pharrell Williams – 'Happy'

The Foundations – 'Build Me Up Buttercup'

The Beach Boys – 'Good Vibrations'

Journey – 'Don't Stop Believin''

What's your happy playlist? Write your own happy playlist and remember to share the love ♥ and tunes on social media! #BeCoolBeNice

10 FRIENDSHIP POINTS

SOMEONE WHO:

1. is loyal

2. is kind to you and others

3. lifts you up instead of brings you down

4. brings you joy (makes you laugh out loud)

5. knows your secrets and keeps them secret

6. knows your bad side but brings out your good side

7. makes you want to do better, feel better, be better

   without making you feel lesser

8. celebrates you and lets you celebrate them

9. makes you feel like you are number one

10. is fun on the run

(REMEMBER . . . IF SHE'S TALKING ABOUT THEM, SHE'S TALKING ABOUT YOU TOO BOO) YOUR VIBE ATTRACTS YOUR TRIBE

BE YOU BE COOL BE NICE

#BeCoolBeNice

Cool Friends

✏️ Write a list of your coolest and nicest friends and acquaintances.

BCBN Bestie

Pick your bestie and take a selfie with the BCBN Bestie Banner on the BCBN app menu. Share your photo on social and the reasons why your bestie IS the best of all!

Now that's a cool selfie!

#SelfieLove

BE COOL BE NICE

TEST YOUR BESTIE 👫

Friendship works both ways . . . swap your BCBN book with your besties, fill out the below questions and put your friendship to the test! Who really knows who?

What is my full name?

When is my birthday?

What's my eye color?

What are my social media usernames?

What's my favorite color?

What's my favorite movie?

What's my favorite book?

What's my favorite food?

What was my first pet's name?

Who was my first crush?

Film your bestie test and share on social media . . .
Gift BCBN books to all your friends and share the fun! 😎

FRIENDS FORESIGHT

A best friend doesn't just know your story, they help you write it.

Do you and your bestie have a sixth sense? Swap each other's *Be Cool Be Nice* book and both draw the first thing that comes to mind. Once complete, swap and see if you match! #sharing-is-caring

MAKE MAGIC

List all of your magical qualities; don't forget all the big and little things. Whatever makes you unique, celebrate it!

Now that is done, make a list of all the magical qualities of your friends and loved ones. Keep adding to the list and share with them on their birthday, or a special occasion, or Monday, or Tuesday, or Saturday or...

DON'T BOTTLE THINGS UP

Fill the BCBN bottle below with your fears and insecurities and use the BCBN app to smash them!

SELF SILHOUETTE

It's not who you are that holds you back, it's who you think you are. Using only positive words, fill your silhouette with words you associate with yourself. Now do the same for a friend or relative and give them a confidence boost! Share on social!

MAGNIFI-CENCE

Use the BCBN app to use the magnifying glass and see the hidden message from Cool Leo!

Admire and Inspire

Who inspires you? Stick in their picture and write the reasons why you admire them. How can you emulate those qualities yourself?

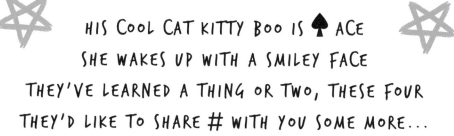

HIS COOL CAT KITTY BOO IS ♠ ACE
SHE WAKES UP WITH A SMILEY FACE
THEY'VE LEARNED A THING OR TWO, THESE FOUR
THEY'D LIKE TO SHARE # WITH YOU SOME MORE...

KITTY BOO LA LA
AKA COOL CAT
KITTY BOO

Conflict Prevention Intention

BCBN TIPS FOR CONFLICT-FREE COMMUNICATION:

Mind your tone (keep your cool)
Mind your manners (as a rule)
Mind your language (you have lost the argument
once you swear or shout)
Mind your volume (keep it level without a doubt)
Mind your stance (body language with no aggression)
Mind your mouth (before your words
cause hypertension)

Listen before you speak
Think before you freak😣
Pause before you act🎭
Stop before you attack👊

Walk away when the pressure rises
That way there's no bad surprises

You can be passionate and still be compassionate♥

We have to reinstate the social contract🤝
of how we treat each other
Without it, we are lost forever

We don't always have to agree, but we do always
have to agree to...

Be Cool Be Nice
Not just once not just twice
With everything you do or say
Kindness takes you all the way

#NuffSaidForReal

The fun is not quite done!

Spot Honey Bee Cool throughout your copy of BCBN (12 times).
He may be small but he sure is sweet. **#BeCivil**

Also, please don't forget to share your beautiful coloring pages and
other cool BCBN creativity pages using the hashtag **#BeCoolBeNice**

If you think someone needs to brush up on their cool and nice manners,
give them the BCBN book with the appropriate pages marked (nicer way
of letting them know to check it b4 they wreck it ☺)
If someone has been cool and nice, give them the BCBN book as a thank
you and share the love - not just once, not just twice . . . .

U.S. ANTI-BULLYING RESOURCES

Bystander Revolution
bystanderrevolution.org

Kind Campaign
kindcampaign.com

The Cybersmile Foundation
cybersmile.org

Stomp Out Bullying
stompoutbullying.org

Ditch the Label
us.ditchthelabel.org

WE Movement
we.org

DISCLAIMER

DEDICATION

Very Special Thanks to my Godchildren and God's children for inspiring this project;

Zoe Kravitz, Noa, Ina kai, Naima, Kami, Moani, Hiro and Sola Laliberte, Louis, Carlo and Lucca Mole, Sharif, Jamil and Zahara Jibrilu, Madison and Dimitri Deveaux, Noemie, Savannah and Romeo Lovas, Anaïs Gallagher, Rob & Alex Keith, Charlie & Savannah Murphy, Ariel Trazzi Hennink.

Very Special Thanks to the awesomely cool and nice Charlotte Stockdale and Katie Lyall at Chaos Fashion and the incomparable Rosie Lyall for bringing their Chaos Fashion cool and nice visual magic.

Huge Thank You also to the wonderfully cool and nice creative artists and designers who so beautifully contributed their artistry; especially Master BCBN graphic designer Dan Sheffield and BCBN chief of digital Gabriel Lovas, Christopher Bailey and Burberry, Marc Jacobs, Alber Elbaz, Emilio Pucci, Peter Dundas, Henry Holland, Pat McGrath, Lenny Kravitz and Kirsten Mattila at Kravitz Design, Neil Barrett, Mary Katrantzou, Katie Grand, Daniella Helayel, Dan & Dean Caten and Dsquared2, Jona Cerwinske, Hattie Stewart, Ivo Bisignano, Pierre LaGrange and Huntsman, Arianne Phillips, Jamie Hewlett, Violante Nessi, Francesca Amfitheatrof, Remi Paringaux, Ben Gorham & Byredo, Sofi Azais, Valentin Milou, Mathieu Bitton, Fritz Kok, Colette and super huge thanks to the incomparable Marc Newson.

Kylie Minogue, Dacha Zhukova and the wonderful team at *Garage* Magazine, Ben Scherwin, Ty Blachly and the wonderful team at Snapchat, Nicolas Newbold, Lorenzo Martone, Char de Francesco, Phil Poynter, Piergiorgio Del Moro, Samuel Ellis Scheinman, Dorothea Hodge, Tiina Saukko, Beris Gwynne, Brittany Stewart, Hanna Benjamin, Brandt Pilgrim, Matt Setchell, Melika Imoru, Marpessa Hennink, Claudia Barila, Salvo Nicosia, Patrick Cox, David Furnish, Sir Elton John, Andreas Zehntner, Sophie Conran, Jasper Conran, Hugh Wahla, Stephen Briars and all at the Conran Shop, Vanessa Paradis.

Very Special Thanks To The Beautifully Cool And Nice June Sarpong, Joy Jibrilu, Lord Alli, Baroness McDonagh, Baroness Scotland, Baroness Amos, Fee Bradshaw, Marita Stavrou, Jeanette Calliva, Tania Bryer, Heather Kerzner, Cynthia Garrett, Lisa Bonet, Dr Evadney Keith, Rev Dr Kenris Carey, Roxie Roker, Kevin Carey, Cheryl Carey, Levarity & Judy Deveaux, Audrey Deveaux, Connie Munnings, Earl & BJ Deveaux, Deveral Ferguson, Steve Deveaux, Kim Sawyer, Cindy Munnings, Pip, Ben & Will Simmons, St Michael's Boyd Subdivision Nassau, Bahamas, from whence the cool and nice lessons came.

The Superbly Cool And Nice Christopher Little, Naomi Campbell, Edward Enninful, Jeff Hafer, Christian Bunke, Michelle Pindling, Claire Hepburn, Charles Carter, Jules Bearman, Emma Schlesinger, Cathy King, Jenna Adler, David Maisel, Guy Laliberté, Natalie Massenet, Veronica Webb, Michael Foster, Douglas Chabbott and the Chabbott family, Arnaud Massenet, Marisa Peer, Mark Itkin, Bradley Bayou, Amir Shahkhalili, Nicola Stephenson, Clara Spahr, Kaylee Conley, Jacob Stetson, Katy Hall, Mission PR, Jane Neale, Nell Cundle, Khaled Al Muhairy, TK Khan, Ebs Burnough, Gelila And Wolfgang Puck, Camilla Olson, Andreas Carlsson, Patrice and Precious Motsepe, Simon And Michaela de Pury, Barbara Becker, Jay Jopling, Camilla Al Fayed, Kim Hersov, Jenny Halpern, Fru Tholstrup, Tamara Mellon, Elizabeth Saltzman, Amanda Kyme, Yassmin Ghandehari, Karla Otto and all at Karla Otto, Vanessa von Bismarck, Daniel Marks and the Communication Store, Michael & Sue Gudinski, Jane & Jimmy Barnes, Jepi & Mark Lizotte, Amanda Mahoney, Darren Dalton, Machteld van Gelder, Frans Monsma, Nico van der Helm, Edwin Peeters, Winston Gerschtanowitz, Chris Zegers, Marc Prosman, Karim Masri, Ana Paula Junqueira, Quohnos Mitchell, Bill Coleman, Ultra Naté, Ben Frow, Mark Gibb.

Zues Sherlock, Jonathan Stambolis, David Ohana, Jonnie Goodwin, Brent Hoberman, Poppy Gaye, Adam Townsend, Mervyn Lyn, Peter Dubens, Carla Bowden, Jess Brown and Saskia Harper at Glue Creative, Perminder Mann, Helen Wicks, Amy Llambias and the wonderful team at Bonnier UK. Shimul Tolia, Sonali Fry, Gayley Avery and the wonderful team at Bonnier USA. Simon & Schuster, Huge thanks to the wonderful Al MacCuish and the Sunshine Company, Kerry Taylor and Viacom, Ben Frow, Simon Franks, Glenn Brawn & Redbus Media, Lisa Goodchild, Chandni Modha, Julie Evans, Graham Bird and MPC, John Genovese, Damian Mould, William Plane, Felipe Noriega, Carlo Barone, Manny Ezugwu, Meg Matthews, Omer Karacan, Dimitri Fisun.

Navid Mirtorabi, Imogen Weiss, Craig Fruin, Howard Kaufman, Sunna Lee, Stonebridge, Mikkel & Tor/Stargate, Adam ADL Baptiste, Alex Strehl, Britta Bergström, Craig Ross, Harold Todd, Ray Moody, Jocelyn Cooper, Lisa Cortes, Elizabeth Manice, Elizabeth Von Guttman, Ömer Karacan, Gustavo Antonioni, Poalo Sella, Melissa Odabash, Sharliss Asbury, DJ Ruckus, Jovar Andrews, Kelly Bostwick, Lisa Bostwick, Carol Abe, Benny Medina, LA Reid, Sylvia Rhone, Rodney Burns, Matthew Morgan & Afropunk, Lola Mercier, Federico Giammarusto, Larissa Giers, Gerlinde Höbel, Vito Ingrosso, Marcus von Euler, Bjorn Lendin, Julia Record, Charlie Mole & Sarah McDonald, Stephanie Dorance, Martyn Lawrence Bullard, Martin Smith, Mark Amadei.

FRITZ KOK

VERY SPECIAL THANK YOU TO...

MARC NEWSON

BURBERRY

MARC JACOBS

LENNY KRAVITZ
KRAVITZ DESIGN

PAT MCGRATH

EMILIO PUCCI

NEIL BARRETT

DSQUARED2

ALBER ELBAZ

CHAOS FASHION

ARIANNE PHILLPS
X JAMIE HEWLETT

KATIE GRAND

MARY KATRANTZOU

HUNTSMAN

HENRY HOLLAND

HATTIE STEWART

JONA CERWINSKE

FRANCESCA
AMFITHEATROF

DANIELLA HELAYEL

IVO BISIGNANO

VIOLANTE NESSI

MATHIEU BITTON

REMI PARINGAUX

CONRAN TCS

HUGE SPECIAL THANKS TO OUR WONDERFUL BCBN SUPPORTERS AND BIG THANKS FOR THE COOL AND NICE BCBN SHOUT-OUTS FROM:

HRH Princess Beatrice, HRH Princess Eugenie,
@CaraDelevingne, @PixieLott, @Doutzen, @KendallJenner, @C.Syresmith,
@iamNaomiCampbell, @Donatella_Versace, @JourdanDunn, @JoanSmalls, @Taylor_Hill,
@HaileyBaldwin, @GigiHadid, @BellaHadid, @RitaOra, @AdwoaAboah, @MissKarenElson,
@WinnieHarlow, @StellaMaxwell, @AmberValletta, @NatashaPoly, @YasminLeBon,
@Emrata, @ErinOConnor, @iosonoMariacarlaBoscono, @SaraSampaio, @AdrianaLima,
@iamMariaBorges, @FeiFeiSun, @SofiaRichie, @AliceOliviaDellalxiii, @Charlotte_Olympia,
@AndreaDellal, @MadisonBeer, @LuckyBSmith, @StormiBree, @AustinMahone,
@BrandonThomasLee, @Rocky_Barnes, @JordanBarrett, @JacquelineF143;
@SonamaKapoor, @DialaMakki, @Anna_Dello_Russo, @ZhenyaKatava, @LukasAbbat,
@DidierDrogba, @Miss_JAlexander, @EmmaGannonuk, @PointlessBlog

THANK YOU!

GRATITUDE SHARING CHALLENGE EXAMPLES:
(FROM PAGES 66 & 67)

- What friend are you grateful for today and why?
  (can be more than one, then let them know, share the love on social, pass it on)
- What family member are you grateful for today and why?
  (can be more than one, then let them know, share the love, pass it on)
- What are you grateful for today when you wake up?
- What sound are you grateful for today?
- What vision are you grateful for today?
- What smell are you grateful for today?
- What song are you grateful for today?
- What small thing are you grateful for today?
- What big thing are you grateful for today?
- What happened today that you are grateful for?
- What happened this week that you are grateful for?
- What dream or aspiration are you grateful for today?
- Who or what that is helping you reach that goal are you grateful for today?
- What mentor are you grateful for today?
- What talents that you have are you grateful for today?
- What talents of a friend or family are you grateful for today? (then share and let them know)
- What is something that your family does that you are grateful for today?
  (then share and let them know)
- What is something that an acquaintance does that you are grateful for today?
- What is something that your bestie does that you are grateful for today?
- What act of kindness from a stranger are you grateful for today?
- What act of kindness from yourself are you grateful for today?
- What challenge are you grateful for today?
- What unique characteristics of yourself are you grateful for today?
- What unique characteristics of your bestie are you grateful for today?
- Which loyal person are you grateful for today?
- Which kind person are you grateful for today?
- Which forgiving and understanding person are you grateful for today?
- Which thoughtful person are you grateful for today?
- What gift from the universe are you grateful for today?
- What lesson are you grateful for today?
- What wisdom are you grateful for today?

THANK YOU CHAOS FASHION!

Q. Social media has made it incredibly easy to bully people. What would your message be to all the trolls and cyber bullies?

CS: Be very, very, careful before you press the send button. You cannot erase your words once out there. The consequences can cause extreme harm to those you are mean to and great harm therefore, to yourself.
KL: You never know what someone else might be going through or struggling with and what takes a second to type can hurt the recipient for so much longer... It's easy to be a faceless bully - which makes you a coward. What takes far more courage is having the confidence to be kind face to face... that should be the goal.

Q. What is a kindness/good manners tool that you learned that would also be valuable for others?

CS: Put yourself in the position of the other person before you judge. Try to see both sides clearly.
KL: Win with kindness and don't lose your head... even in the face of an angry or rude person. You will disarm them and always come out on top. You also won't live to regret your words or actions.

Q. How do you think we can all improve being cool and nice in our daily lives?

CS: Ironically, I think you need to love yourself. Not in a narcissistic way. But be at peace with yourself. Attempt not only to be the best at what you do, but the best that you can be to others. Find your values and stick to them. Know that people who make you challenge your values are not valuable to you. Stay true. It's not easy! Remember to live by the rule - be to others how you would like them to be to you.
KL: I think that simple manners go a very long way. Please, thank you and starting with how are you is always recommended and appreciated.

Q. Have you or someone you know ever been bullied? How did this make them/you feel?

CS: I was bullied for three years at boarding school. It changed the direction of my life because I gave up subjects I loved like art to avoid this girl. It was miserable. I dreamed of having superpowers so I could frighten her or hurt her - obviously wrong. Then one day I just had enough. I suddenly realised I just mustn't and shouldn't care. And only by confronting her would I get past this pointless and painful barrier to my life and happiness. I found her and told her I thought she was sad, small and mean. That I felt sorry for her, because she must be so unhappy to be so unkind. Her jaw dropped and she never bothered me again. I felt both elated and so angry that it took so much courage and pain to gather that courage and belief in myself, and it took two minutes to undo three years of torture. But in the end I moved on.

KL: There have been so many moments in my life when the words or actions of others have caused me to feel sad, insecure and doubt myself. Some huge and some tiny... but they add up and stay with you. Sometimes people know when they do it and I guess often it's not intentional but knocks away at your confidence anyway. It happens through school and continues to happen in your adult life. When it all adds up, it's sometimes quite difficult to clear your head and remember your worth but try you must.

Q. What advice would you give them/yourself now?

CS: 30 years on, I know to try and confront things as they happen... It takes so much courage and focus. I fail a lot still!
KL: I would remind myself that what people think of you and the way that people treat you is often a reflection of their own insecurities. Try to not sweat the small stuff and remember the bigger picture and focus on your goals and inspirations to stay on track. Then the little things that could weigh you down become irrelevant.

Q. How would being cool and nice have affected/changed that experience?

CS: Hmm. Being cool would have meant I could have recognised that her behaviour came from pain. I think that people can be mean because they are really not nice, but it must start from their own insecurities 99% of the time. The first thing to look for when someone is mean is whether this comes from simple true meanness or whether that person actually is very, very unhappy.

Q. Chaos have been amazing first supporters of Be Cool Be Nice; what made you want to support Be Cool Be Nice?

CS: Because we believe. Be Cool Be Nice is the greatest message.
KL: Because there is no other way to be... and those confused about that need to know!

Q. Who are the coolest and nicest people you know (historical or otherwise)?

CS: Jo Allison, Alice Bamford and Wendy Rowe.
KL: Dave Lyall, Evie Hall.

Q. What four positive words would you use to describe yourself?
Kindness. Giving. Patience. (Be) Honourable. Hmmmmmmmmmmmmm, trying, not always succeeding, at being the person I know I ought to be.
Positive, Loyal, Dedicated, Silly.
KL:

CHARLOTTE STOCKDALE & KATIE LYALL

Thank You!

LILAKOI MOON

JUNE SARPONG

KYLIE MINOGUE

DAN SHEFFIELD

STARGATE

ROSIE LYALL

CHARLOTTE STOCKDALE

KATIE LYALL

PERMINDER MANN & THE BONNIER UK TEAM

DOROTHEA HODGE

AL MACCUISH & THE SUNSHINE COMPANY

NAOMI CAMPBELL

SIMON & SCHUSTER

SONALI FRY

GAYLEY AVERY

JONNIE GOODWIN

VANESSA VON BISMARC

SHIMUL TOLIA & THE BONNIER USA TEAM

VICKY SANZ

GARAGE MAGAZINE

MATTHEW MORGAN & AFROPUNK

BARBARA BECKER

JEANETTE CALLIVA

HEATHER KERZNER

ANA PAULA JUNQUEIRA

CHRISTIAN BUNKE

CATHY KING

FEE BRADSHAW

TIFFANIE DARKE

ERROLL DOUGLAS

SALVO NICOSIA

BARONESS SCOTLAND

MICHAEL FOSTER

MARPESSA HENNINK

NELL CUNDLE

MISSION MEDIA

AMY LLAMBIAS

KAREN CUMMINGS PALMER

JENNY HALPERN & RYAN PRINCE

MICHAELA & SIMON DE PURY

JOY JIBRILU

GELILA AND WOLFGANG PUCK

HELEN WICKS

MARISA PEER

CAMILLA AL FAYED

SOPHIE CONRAN

LORD ALLI

FRU THOLSTRUP

ELIZABETH SALTZMAN

FEDERICO GIAMMARUSTO

CARLA BOWDEN, JESS BROWN & SASKIA HARPER AT GLUE CREATIVE

ST. MICHAELS NASSAU, BAHAMAS

BRITTA BERGSTRÖM

ADAM ADL BAPTISTE

DAVID OHANA

CAMILLA OLSSON

DASHA ZHUKOVA

DR. LISA AIRAN & DR. TREVOR BORN

REBECCA MARTINEZ

PIERRE LAGRANGE

THE ROYAL FOUNDATION

CAROL ABE

TARIQ TK KHAN

LISA BOSTWICK

SARAH MANLEY

KHALED AL MUHAIRY

BEN SCHWERIN, TY BLACHLY AND ALL OUR COOL AND NICE FRIENDS AT SNAPCHAT

NATALIE IMBRUGLIA

PATRICK COX

MARITA STAVROU

CHARLIE MOLE & SARAH MCDONALD

PIERGIORGIO DEL MORO

MELISSA ODABASH

MARTYN LAWRENCE BULLARD

140

ANAÏS GALLAGHER
MEG MATTHEWS

MARTIN SMITH

PRINCESS BEATRICE

SOFI AZAÏS

MELIKA IMORU

VERONICA WEBB

RODNEY BURNS

BEN GORHAM & BYREDO

NATALIE MASSENET

LARISSA GIERS

SIMON FRANKS AND ALL AT REDBUS

BILL COLEMAN

MARK AMADEI

JEFF HAFER

VALENTIN MILOU

JOHN GENOVESE

STONEBRIDGE

ULTRA NATÉ

JULIE EVANS, GRAHAM BIRD & MPC

BARONESS AMOS

LISA GOODCHILD

RAY MOODY

VITO INGROSSO

DANIEL MARKS

MICHELLE PINDLING

BENNY MEDINA

SAMUEL ELLIS PRINCESS EUGENIE

VIOLANTE NESSI

PAOLO SELLA

DAVID MAISEL

JOCELYN COOPER

LOLA MERCIER

ARNAUD MASSENET

ZUES SHERLOCK

PHIL POYNTER

COLETTE PARIS

JENNA ADLER

ALICIA VALENCIA

ZOE KRAVITZ

UNICEF

CLAUDIA BARILA

BARONESS MCDONAGH

CHANDNI MODHA

KELLY BOSTWICK

TAMARA MELLON

KIRSTEN MATTILA

BRADLEY BAYOU

WILLOW SMITH

KENDALL JENNER

CRAIG FRUIN & SUNNA LEE

CHRISTOPHER LITTLE

CRAIG ROSS

JANE NEALE

POPPY GAYE

CHAR DEFRANCESCO

DANNY D POKU

KERRY TAYLOR & VIACOM

BRENT HOBERMAN AND FOUNDERS FORUM

MARK ITKIN

ABUAKWA SIAW-MISA

PIP, WILL & BEN SIMMONS

NICO VAN DER HELM

LA REID

MATT COYSTON

WILLIAM PLANE

KÖNRAD BERGSTROM AND ZOUND INDUSTRIES

NAVID MIRTORABI

NICOLAS NEWBOLD

DAMIAN MOULD

SYLVIA RHONE

SERENA GOH

DR. EVADNEY KEITH

ANDREAS CARLSSON

LISA MANICE

KARLA OTTO

EDWARD ENNINFUL

STEPHANIE DORRANCE

DAVID FURNISH

VANESSA PARADIS

GUY LALIBERTÉ

141

AS YOU WOULD
HAVE DONE TO YOU
UNTO OTHERS
SAME BE TRUE
JUST BEFORE
YOU CLOSE THE DEAL
ASK, HOW WOULD
THIS MAKE ME FEEL?

LEO LOVINGTONS IS BEYOND COMPARE
HE REALLY IS AN ★ AWESOME BEAR
HIS FRIENDS THEY CALL HIM COOL LEO
THE KIND OF BEAR YOU'D WANT TO KNOW...

LEO LOVINGTONS

AKA COOL LEO

HIS BEST ★ MATE
FRU LA RUE IS FAB
THE BEST FRIEND ♥
YOU 👤 COULD EVER HAVE...

FRU LA RUE
AKA FRU FRU

#FruRealness

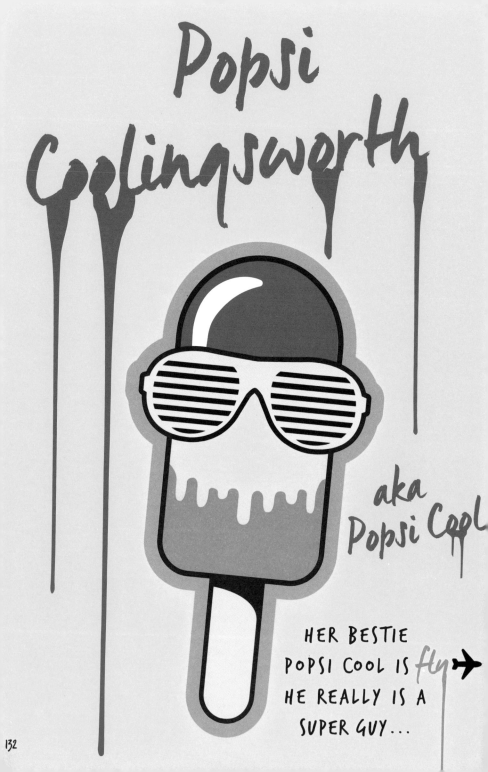

Popsi Coolingsworth

aka
Popsi Cool

HER BESTIE
POPSI COOL IS *fly* ✈
HE REALLY IS A
SUPER GUY...